THE WISHING TREE

by
Emalie Alaniz and Manuel Cota

AuthorHouse™
1663 Liberty Drive
Bloomington, IN 47403
www.authorhouse.com
Phone: 833-262-8899

Because of the dynamic nature of the Internet, any web addresses or links contained in this book may have changed since publication and may no longer be valid. The views expressed in this work are solely those of the author and do not necessarily reflect the views of the publisher, and the publisher hereby disclaims any responsibility for them.

Any people depicted in stock imagery provided by Getty Images are models, and such images are being used for illustrative purposes only. Certain stock imagery © Getty Images.

This book is printed on acid-free paper.

ISBN: 978-1-6655-6562-2 (sc)
ISBN: 978-1-6655-6563-9 (e)

Print information available on the last page.

Published by AuthorHouse 10/07/2022

authorHOUSE

Hello, My name is Manuel Cota,
And I'am a Covid-19 Survivor. Early of January of 2021, I contracted the disease. It took me 11 months to recover, 4 1/2 months in the hospital and 4 1/2 months in rehab Center. As I started to write an adult book about my Journey. That all soon change to a children book, In-hope that they would have an understanding to my journey. Our book is, a mixture of me and my 8 year old great-grand-daughter as we collaborated on the book together and along with some illustration that we created. I welcome her participation for the only reason, she was a witness to my Journey, other then my wife. She said that she was happy and glad that I was home and her wish had come true. I asked her about her wish and she replied that she made it to my Wishing Tree that sits on my desk. That's when I decided to express my connection with my tree as myself and my Journey.

The story of The Wishing Tree.

To my great granddaughter, Little Ricky represents her Little Brother. For me and others, it represent my wife, and all the professional that took care of me at the hospital and rehab center and order for me to survive. At one point at my stay at the hospital they inform my wife that I was not going to make it. Imagine that, receiving a call, and informing you, that you're not going to be able to see or talk to the one you love, and or say you last goodbye. I asked my wife, how possibly I could had survive. And she replied, It was, because I was blessed and love by many and the thousands of prayers that I received from family and friends. Please don't be thinking that I have replace the good Lord with my tree. The good Lord will always be number one and in my book. The power of prayer is the one thing that got me through this ordeal and is the best medicine that anyone could receive. Believe me or not the power of prayer is very strong.

Thank you Lord, to listening to all of those prayers, so I can live to see on another day, Amen.

By Emalie Alaniz and Manuel Cota

In my great-grandfathers room on his desk,
There is one special tree, and I called it,
The Wishing Tree.

If you can find it, Make a wish.
If you make a wish, Your wish could come true

Once upon a time, there was a little boy, named Ricky.
Who lived in the deepest part of the Forest.

In the deepest part of the Forest.
There was one special tree, which he call,

 The Wishing Tree.

When ever Little Ricky was unhappy,
He enjoy visiting The Wishing Tree, Why?

Because, it made him very happy.

So, one day, he told The Wishing Tree.
If you should ever fall.
I will take care of you for ever.

So one day he saw that all
around The Wishing Tree.
Trees were falling.
So Little Ricky asked The Wishing Tree,
Why are all these trees falling?

And The Wishing Tree replied to Little Ricky.

You see, we got this disease,

Where it came from,

No one knows?

And how it looks like,

No one knows?

No one knows?

Rather you are Young or Old, And Weak or Strong,
It didn't matter who you are?

Mother nature give us a test to see,
Who could survive.

So I like to leave a few words to the wise.
That have stood the test of time.

So keep reading my story from time to time.
As I try to explain to understand why?

My life's journey has been a long road in time.

I was tested time after time.

Because you see, my spirit runs down deep,
Running through Way beneath my feet.

The strong rain may have stole my fir away.
And as the mighty winds may have flown night and day.

I pray and pray and fought you back to find a way. So I could live to see another day.

So, the weary wind gave up and spoke.

And I replied.

I fought you back and held my ground,

While other trees were falling.

Because of my roots they are stretch into the earth,
Growing stronger and stronger
Since my birth.

You never touched them,
For you see, My roots are the deepest Part of me.

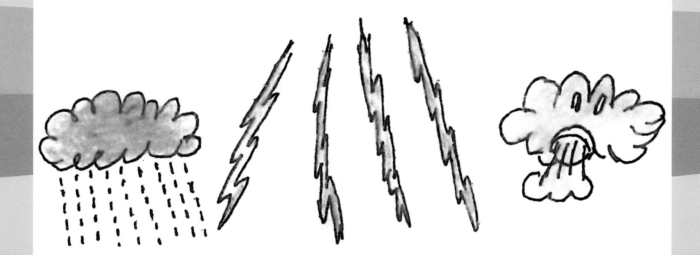

Until today, I wasn't sure,
On how much I could endure.

And thanks to you and to the lord, I found out,
I am stronger now, Than I ever knew.

And thanks to you, Is the reason why,
I am still standing Because of you.

THE WISHING TREE

So try to remember,
How special you truly are.

So keep Praying, Dreaming, And Hoping
That I can make your wish come, True.

Grandpa
Manuel Cota & Emaile Alaniz

wishing you a very
MERRY CHRISTMAS

The Wishing Tree

The Wishing Tree.

FOOTNOTE.

Thank you for taking your time to read our book. We hope that you enjoy it as much as we enjoy making it. As I mention before, what started out to an adult book, that soon change to a children's book. It was requested by my Great grand daughter. So children her age might have an understanding of my journey. I plan to continue finishing my book so I can explain in detail to an adult, why my world is turn upside down. To have a better understanding of my journey, I will reveal the Shocking Analysis of my six months after my release. My suspicion on my condition was verified by my therapist. To Most of all of you, you must think I am cure and that is far from the truth. I am struggling with a certain Health condition as of now. To some of you, you may be thinking that I come to my end of my road, but to be honest with you, it's only the beginning.

—Manuel

Printed in the United States
by Baker & Taylor Publisher Services